Rockstar Bob

Here is a collection of 136 ideas for rockstar employee engagement. Some are quite specific, others are quite broad. Some will work in your particular business environment, others won't. Some you'll be able to afford, others you won't. Some will work together, others won't. Some will be easy, others will be difficult. Some might be one-time things, others might become tradition. Some may work across the entire business, others may only work in one area. Some ideas you'll hate and think are totally stupid, others you'll fall in love with (hopefully), Some are big projects, others are small. Some are silly, others are practical. Some will have a massive impact, others only a little. You might want to implement all of the ideas, you might only want to implement one.

Either way, all will bring a smile to your rockstars faces and make them feel closer and more connected to each other, your company and your customers.

What is a 'Rockstar Employee'?

A 'Rockstar Employee' is one that excels in their field. They are brave and bold, they are empowered and open, they have fun and sometimes take a few risks, everything they do is for the fan (customer). They experiment, they trust their bandmates, they value their crew. They stand out, they are individual, they are unique. They improvise, they like to party, they collaborate, they communicate…to summarize…
THEY ROCK!

Anyone can be a rockstar in whatever they do, they don't need to play an instrument, sing, or even throw TV's out of hotel room windows (even though that is fun). All they need is a certain attitude and outlook about who they are and what they do. All they need is for someone to engage and awaken their inner rockstar. Understand and act on this and you will have a company full of rockstar employees delivering rockstar results.

This book will give you 136 ideas to create and nurture that 'Rockstar Employee Engagement'

#1

Commit to creating 'Rockstar Employee Engagement' by
assigning an 'Employee Engagement' budget.

#2

Your employees are rockstars, let them meet the fans. Have them meet the customers and/or end users of their product or service and hear how the company's products and services effect customers lives.

#3

When an employee performs like a rockstar, send some fan mail to their family explaining what they have done, how valuable they are to the company and how proud they should be of them.

#4

Have 'CEO Time' where the CEO grabs a drink with an
employee who has done rockstar work to praise and discuss.

#5

Giving shares in the company to all employees
(even if it's just a small amount) drives extreme engagement
and knowing that they own a little bit of the company makes
them feel like an absolute rockstar.

#6

Increase trust, responsibility and empowerment by giving employees a discretionary budget to fix mistakes, add value or to apologize to customers like a rockstar.

#7

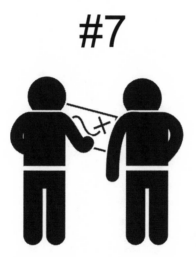

Rockstar employees see themselves reflected in their company's core values. Create your rockstar values with your employees.

#8

Promote autonomy and value buy-in by allowing employees to use core values to help them make empowered rockstar decisions.

#9

Rockstars have a purpose. Help your employees feel like rockstars by working with them to define your company mission/purpose.

#10

Making sure all employees know how their work contributes towards the company mission/purpose will help them get through even the toughest of gigs.

#11

All big bands were once little bands with a vision. Create your company vision with your employees.

#12

Ensure commitment and understanding by making sure that every employee knows and understands how being a rockstar contributes towards achieving the vision of the company.

#13

For displaying our
rockstar values
$50

Reinforce your rockstar values by having bonus and reward
programs that recognize employees for displaying your
rockstar values.

#14

Reinforce your rockstar values by basing performance reviews around the values.

#15

Allow employees to see a progression path and work towards
a goal by giving everyone in the organization a rockstar
learning and development plan.

#16

Decrease stress and show trust by allowing employees to choose their own working hours. Rockstars sometimes like to sleep in.

#17

Change mind-sets about work by changing job titles to reflect your culture. "Customer Experience Rockstar" for example.

#18

Even rockstars get sick. Effectively use time and promote wellness by having a company doctor that all employees can use.

#19

Rockstars demand food and drink in their dressing rooms.
Promote health and wellbeing by giving subsidized or free
healthy food.

#20

Encourage autonomy and show trust by empowering
employees to make decisions without asking for permission.
Rockstars don't ask for permission.

#21

Rockstars rely on their bandmates. Implement a buddy rule. If an employee has an idea about how to fix a problem for a customer, rather than asking a manager, they just have to get the nod from another employee.

#22

Have periodic themed dress up days. Superhero day, Film star day, even rockstar day.

#23

Instill a sense of pride in your workforce by holding a 'get to know the company' family fun day where employees bring their families to work and they learn about the company. Rockstars have families too you know.

#24

Build a strong and connected team by taking them out to films, meals, bowling, etc. A band that plays together, stays together.

#25

Help employees use their time effectively by having a concierge service to help them book restaurant tables, cinema or theatre tickets etc. Treat them like a real rockstar.

#26

Promote transparency and openness by holding regular forums or 'jam sessions' as I like to call them that encourage employees to speak up.

#27

Have regular time slots where employees can ask any question they like to the executive team and get open, honest and transparent answers. Rockstars need to know what's going on at the record label.

#28

Promote organic interdepartmental collaboration by holding cross department away days and events to help your rockstar employees get to know each other better.

#29

Inject fun and recognition by making, and encouraging others to make random rockstar awards for people from paper plates and cups etc.

#30

Show commitment to your employees growth by getting coaches and mentors for them to help with their professional, personal and rockstar development.

#31

Encourage interdepartmental collaboration by regularly putting cross department teams together for projects. Think of it like forming a rockstar super-group.

#32

Encourage employees to grow as people not just as workers by giving rockstar education opportunities to them that don't necessarily directly benefit your company.

#33

Boost morale and keep energy high by playing music at work…preferably heavy metal.

#34

Make employees feel comfortable at work by having a relaxed dress policy. Rockstars wear what they want.

#35

Help your rockstars connect with the CEO/President on a human level by starting a CEO/President blog.

#36

Encourage pride in the company by facilitating and sponsoring opportunities for employees to be rockstars in the community. Cleaning up neighborhoods, feeding the homeless, donating blood for example.

#37

Let employees feel like they are part of something bigger by allocating money to be donated to charity. Let them vote on which charities will benefit and distribute accordingly. Rockstars like to give back.

#38

Show employees that you value them and their message by turning them into real rockstars in your marketing material, brochures, TV, radio etc.

#39

Give your employees a 'lighthouse' by creating a simple and powerful mission statement that every employee lives by. Mine is 'Create Rockstars'.

#40

Reduce stress by creating some really cool chill
out spaces or 'green rooms' as they are known
in the biz.

#41

Let your employees know that you care for them beyond the
job by celebrating their birthdays. Rockstars love to party.

#42

Let your employees know you value them by celebrating their joining date anniversary. Rockstars love to party.

#43

Celebrate your employees achievements at work. Landing a
big client or successfully completing a project for example.
Rockstars love to party.

#44

Show genuine care for your employees by celebrating their achievements outside of work. Having a baby or running a marathon for example.
Did I mention that rockstars love to party?

#45

Promote a culture that isn't scared to try new things by
encouraging and even rewarding failure. Rockstars try new
things all the time, this inevitably means messing up every
now and again.

#46

Keep your rockstar's morale up and end the week on a high by bringing in entertainers on Fridays. Musicians, comedians or magicians for example.

#47

Reinforce your mission and promote your brand by putting your logo and mission statement on cool stuff. Hats, t-shirts, bags, yoga mats for example. Rockstars love to brand everything!

#48

Promote your rockstar employee's health and promote your brand by giving employees free branded bicycles to get to work.

#49

Decrease stress and boost creativity with art classes.
Rockstars love to be creative.

#50

Allow employees to find the right path to an outcome by having less process driven work and more outcome driven work. Rockstars love to improvise.

#51

Show recognition and gratitude by holding weekly award ceremonies. It doesn't need to be anything fancy, it could be as simple as a 'Most Rockingest Rockstar' award that gets circulated.

#52

Keep employees informed by starting each day with a 'pre gig' huddle to share company goings-on, celebrate what went well yesterday, discuss what can be improved today and re-inforce the current goals and targets.

#53

Boost morale, promote fun and keep energy high by playing office games. "Work hard, play hard" is the rockstar motto.

#54

Show gratitude and promote team togetherness by having a weekly, company funded, Friday afternoon happy hour. There's only one thing rockstars like more than beer...free beer.

#55

Help new rockstars feel part of the band quickly by taking them for a rockstar night out after their first day.

#56

Invest in your rockstars by training them regularly and well.
Don't cheap out on this. Rockstars don't become rockstars by
accident, they are constantly learning and progressing.

#57

Being a rockstar can be stressful, treat your employees and reduce their stress by occasionally bringing in or hiring a full time massage therapist.

#58

Help your rockstar employees look and feel their best by occasionally bringing in or hiring a full time hair, make-up and nail person so employees can do these time consuming activities onsite.

#59

Promote friendships and connections between your employees by starting special interest groups. Jogging, cycling, football, extreme death metal, chess.

#60

Allow employees to see what happens at the top by starting a 'CEO for the day' program. Rockstar CEOs make rockstar employees.

#61

Promote a healthy work-life balance and show personal life understanding by being mega flexible with personal days. Sometimes a rockstar has to cancel a gig to look after their family.

#62

Show that you care about employees as people by learning about their hobbies and interests and rewarding them with things that reflect these. Football tickets, gig tickets, magazine subscriptions for example.

#63

Promote your unique culture by creating a fun and unique
office workplace décor and theme.

#64

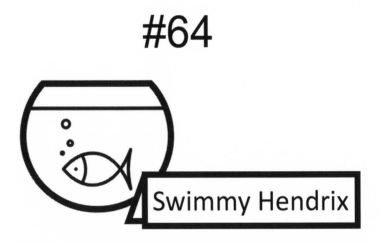

Swimmy Hendrix

Tap into employees emotions by getting an office pet. Even the toughest metal head has a soft spot for animals. Call it something rockstary.

#65

Find employees talents and utilise them, hang employee art and photographs on the walls, get employee musicians to play at meetings, get a pottery rockstar to make mugs for people.

#66

"Master of puppets I'm, pulling your strings"

Showcase your employees unique talents by holding your own "Our Company's Got Talent" talent show.

#67

Get the best work and passion from your employees by discovering what role is best suited to their particular skills and encourage them to work in that area. No good forcing a drummer to play guitar.

#68

Allow your rockstars to blow off steam and have fun by building a bowling alley, basketball court, music room, football pitch or similar at your offices.

#69

Increase your employees potential to learn and network by sending them to lots of conferences, let them choose which ones and encourage them to share what they learned. Every rockstar loves going out on tour.

#70

Let your employees feel like rockstars and share their wisdom
by creating an internal version of TED Talks.

#71

Promote a customer centric workforce by having every employee understand how what they do effects customers. Unfortunately some rockstars think the world revolves around them…show them that it doesn't.

#72

Show appreciation and grow pride by mentioning specific employees by name in press releases. There's nothing more rockstar than being mentioned in the tabloids.

#73

Allow creativity and freedom by allowing time during the day for employees to work on something they are passionate about even if it's not work related…a solo album if you will.

#74

Inject fun, excitement and anticipation by celebrating all holidays from the important and inspiring like 'World Heavy Metal Day' to the crazy and ridiculous like 'National Kazoo Day'.

#75

Even rockstars love a treat. On a particularly hot day get an
ice-cream truck to come to work and give out free
ice-cream.

#76

Show trust in your employees skills by encouraging them to have 'Pet Projects' that they think will benefit the company. Rockstars love the freedom to be creative.

#77

To drive collaboration, set times each month that employees have to work in different departments. This would be like Ozzy Osbourne and Bruce Dickinson swapping places for a show.

#78

Reinforce values by having a weekly reward that employees give to each other for displaying your rockstar values. It has to be cross department and the person who wins has to pick the next winner and share the story.

#79

Promote inclusiveness, contribution and teamwork by having rockstar brainstorming sessions regularly with no judgement or criticism.

#80

Build trust and accountability by having unlimited sick days.
Trust that if they say they're sick, they're sick. Encourage them
to take time off to get better. No rockstar is going to bail on a
gig for no good reason.

#81

Encourage employee health and fitness by creating an onsite gym with showers and changing facilities. Rockstars need to stay in shape.

#82

Connect with employees on a personal level by working hard to work on a first name basis with all employees. Rockstars know their whole crew by name.

#83

When hiring for new roles, look inside of the company before looking outside. This provides employee progression and growth and recognises them for the rockstar they are.

#84

Attract the best rockstars by paying over the average.
Pay average - attract average. When Metallica hired a new
bassist, they gave him a $1,000,000 joining bonus…
just sayin'.

#85

Celebrate your employees achievements like a rockstar by holding a yearly black-tie, red carpet, Oscars style awards night with different work related categories. Let employees vote on winners.

#86

Keep your rockstars motivated by bringing in a recognised motivational speaker every quarter. It can be a professional speaker, musician, athlete, actor, author, whatever.

#87

Hold weekly potluck lunches. Bring your rockstars together to eat and let them show off their culinary skills.

#88

Bring employees into the hiring process. It takes a rockstar to know a rockstar.

#89

Choose a local minor league sports team to support as a company and take everyone to watch them play regularly. Just remember these Pink Floyd lyrics.
"…four-star, daydream, Think I'll buy me a football team."

#90

Have democratic votes on certain executive level decisions.
Rockstars like a say in the decisions that effect them.

#91

Have every member of the top team visit or even better work
on the front line one day a month. Rockstars need to stay
down to earth.

#92

Let your rockstars feel like part of the band by trusting them
with sensitive information at all levels.

#93

Rocktails $5

Metalliquor
Blackberry Sabbath
Jimi Hendrinks
Iron Lemonaiden

Hold a cocktail making class and make company or department signature cocktails. Get them served at your local bar. Give them rockstar names. Rockstars love to feel unique…and they like to drink…did I mention that?

#94

Hold a song writing class, and get each team to write an anthem for their team/department.

#95

Encourage regular breaks for employees to clear their heads
and stretch their legs. Even rockstars need breaks.

#96

Share the board of directors presentation with all employees.

#97

Don't reward or punish your rockstars based on performance reviews. This will encourage true feedback that won't be influenced by reward or punishment.

#98

Hold a yearly office Olympics. Rockstars love a bit of competition.

#99

Drive empowerment and accountability by having employees set their own targets and goals. Rockstars are self starters and know what needs to get done.

#100

Let your rockstars blow off steam. Get board games, foosball, pool tables or even old school arcade machines.

#101

Let your rockstars leave early on sunny/good weather days.
Even rockstars like flying kites.

#102

Have an onsite crèche for the little rockstars of the future.

#103

Have a wall of fame.

#104

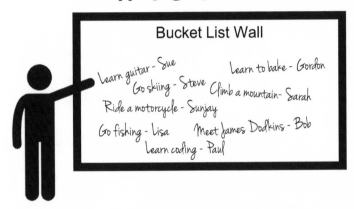

Bucket List Wall

Learn guitar - Sue

Learn to bake - Gordon

Go skiing - Steve

Climb a mountain - Sarah

Ride a motorcycle - Sunjay

Go fishing - Lisa

Meet James Dodkins - Bob

Learn coding - Paul

Have a bucket list board where employees write down things they'd really like to do before they kick it. Encourage other employees to reach out if they can help someone achieve a bucket list item.

#105

Have a 'success bell' that is rung every time there is a
success. everyone cheers...like rockstars.

#106

Ban emails for a day every month, force people to talk to each other face to face. Rockstars need to interact with their band and crew.

#107

Hold 'a day in the life of' days where employees can experience a role in another area of the business that they are interested in or curious about. Rockstars sometimes need to experiment with different genres.

#108

Get office toys like Slinkys and Rubik's cubes. Some say that toys are like heavy metal – the best came out of the 80's

#109

Get a company mascot similar to a sports team that will show up unexpectedly or at events in person. Get something really heavy metal...like a teddy bear.

#110

Share stories of individual and team success. Rockstars love publicity.

#111

Discover which part of an employee's job they dislike the most and figure out a way to ditch it. There's probably another rockstar out there that would love to do it.

#112

Form a culture committee, or 'Culture Club' if you will, to drive rockstar culture focused activities.

#113

Send hand written notes to employees as recognition of good work. Rockstars love fan mail.

#114

Reinforce pride in your company and share progress by
celebrating your company's birthday.
Seriously…any excuse to party

#115

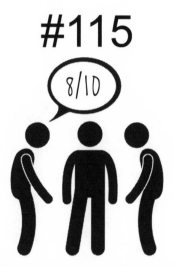

Share feedback from customers with everyone. Rockstars read all album reviews, good and bad.

#116

Recognise top performers by asking them to coach and mentor new hires or people who need an extra bit of help. Rockstars love to pass on their knowledge.

#117

Have job role term limits so people don't stagnate in the same job for years on end. You can only tour for so long on the same album before you've got to write some new material.

#118

Have a 'frustration box' where people can anonymously share their deepest frustrations, make sure you act on the feedback. Some rockstars are shy.

#119

Have epic boxing/wrestling style intros/entrances for new hires
with their own entrance music that the whole office cheer to.
Rockstars love to put on a show.

#120

Add/connect/follow each other on social media. Rockstars like to know what other rockstars are doing.

#121

Give your rockstars loads of hi-fives/fist bumps.

#122

Have all new hires spend a period of time in a customer service role to build a true connection with your customers. You wouldn't hire a new band member if they didn't understand your fans would you?

#123

Allow unlimited vacation as long as peoples work has been finished to the expected standard. That's a real rockstar lifestyle.

#124

Develop your leaders to be better leaders. A band is only as good as their management.

#125

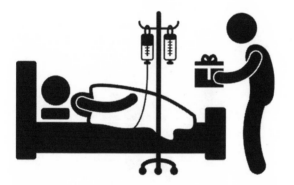

Check up on people who are off sick and send flowers, soup or care packages to show that you care. Even rockstars need to know that you care.

#126

Assign a buddy or mentor for every new hire to help them learn the ropes. New rockstars sometimes get stage fright.

#127

Have an office boxing/wrestling style championship belt that people can win or lose based on performance or some other criteria. Rockstars love awards.

#128

Work on a culture of 'catching people doing the right things' rather than one of 'catching people doing the wrong things'. Only talking about negative things isn't going to get the best out of your rockstars.

#129

Start an internal social media platform where all of your
rockstars can share their rockstar news.

#130

Let employees work from home when they can. More often than not, rockstars are more productive in their pajamas.

#131

Get a company in to wash and clean everyone's cars as a
surprise. A rockstar that travels in style works with style.

#132

Give new hires a 'swag bag' with company branded goodies.
Rockstars love merch.

#133

Put on Christmas parties for employees children.
"Rockin' around the Christmas tree" and so on.

#134

Get rid of cubicles that promote seclusion and have an open plan office that promotes communication and collaboration. Rockstars need to see their bandmates to perform at their best.

#135

Build your hiring criteria in accordance with your company culture, vision, mission and values. Know the exact type of rockstars you want to hire.

#136

Appoint a Chief Culture Officer (or similar) whose job it is to do
these things. Even the best rockstars in the world need
inspiration and guidance.

Get in touch.

If you want fancy talking a little bit more about this stuff,
drop me a line:

Email: jd@rockstar.cx
Website: www.rockstar.cx
Twitter: https://twitter.com/jdodkins
LinkedIn: uk.linkedin.com/in/jamesdodkins
Facebook: http://bit.ly/jamesdodkinsfb
ROCKSTAR CX Facebook Group: http://bit.ly/fbcxgroup

Made in the USA
Middletown, DE
22 August 2023

37158426R00083